Building self-esteem

Helen Jenkins and Melanie Fennell

Oxford Cognitive Therapy Centre
Warneford Hospital
Oxford
OX3 7JX

The advice and information contained in this booklet is the best we can give based on research evidence and clinical experience at the time of writing. However OCTC and the author(s) cannot know the individual circumstances of readers, and therefore cannot accept any liability to readers or others for the consequences of following this advice. If you are in any way uncertain about the best course for you, you should consult your doctor or mental health professional for an individual assessment of your needs.

Building self-esteem

Helen Jenkins and Melanie Fennell

Contents

Contents

1. The nature of low self-esteem

Introduction

This booklet explains how the problem of low self-esteem can affect people, how it develops, and what keeps it going. Practical self-help methods for overcoming low self-esteem are described in detail so that you can learn how to use them yourself. These methods come from ***cognitive behaviour therapy*** (CBT for short). CBT has been found to be an effective treatment for many psychological difficulties, including depression and anxiety problems. This booklet may be useful as a self-help guide whether you are trying to overcome this problem on your own or with professional support.

What is low self-esteem?

Having low self-esteem means having a low opinion of yourself. It affects people in different ways and to different degrees. Most people experience at least some degree of self-doubt in specific situations. For example, this may happen at a job interview or when meeting a new group of people. However, low self-esteem may cause people to lack confidence in many situations, or to dislike themselves in a general way. Common signs of low self-esteem are listed below. As you can see, it can affect thoughts, feelings, body state, behaviour, and relationships.

Thoughts

- self-criticism
- self-blame
- self-doubt
- ignore or discount praise, successes and strengths
- focus on criticisms, mistakes and weaknesses

Feelings

- sadness
- anxiety
- guilt
- shame
- frustration
- anger

Behaviour

- not looking after yourself
- difficulty being assertive and speaking out
- avoiding challenges and opportunities
- shyness, avoiding eye contact, hesitancy
- difficulty making decisions
- perfectionism and working too hard

Body state

- tension
- tiredness
- difficulty sleeping

Relationships

- self-consciousness
- worrying too much about what other people think of you
- trying too hard to please other people
- withdrawal from other people

It may be possible to sum up the negative opinion of yourself in terms of one or two specific beliefs, such as "I'm unlovable", "I'm not good enough", "I'm unacceptable", and so on. In this booklet these fundamental beliefs are referred to as the **Bottom Line** beliefs. They are called this because they are thought to be central to self-esteem, and to have an underlying influence on how we think, feel and behave. It is assumed that we all have **Bottom Line** beliefs, and that these can be positive or negative, accurate or inaccurate. The problem of low self-esteem arises when our **Bottom Line** beliefs are overly negative.

What causes low self-esteem?

Low self-esteem can be seen as an understandable reaction to past experiences. We start to form ideas about ourselves during early childhood based on how other people treat us. These early beliefs continue to be shaped by experiences as we grow up and after we become adults. This means that if another child were to grow up in our shoes and have similar experiences to us, then he or she might develop similar beliefs.

Low self-esteem usually stems from adverse experiences during childhood, but it can also result from bad or traumatic experiences that occur when we are adults. Some people have clear ideas about what caused them to develop low self-esteem, but others find it puzzling. Some of the experiences that commonly lead to low self-esteem are listed below.

- physical, sexual or emotional abuse
- physical or emotional neglect
- rejection
- being bullied
- other traumatic events (e.g. bereavements, being assaulted, accidents, serious illness, losses)
- excessive criticism
- not enough affection or praise
- being different to the people around us
- parents having unrealistic expectations of us
- parents having low self-esteem

Some causes of low self-esteem may be harder to identify than others, and sometimes this can make it difficult to understand where low self-esteem comes from. For instance, the experiences in the bottom half of the list may be harder to identify than those nearer the top. However, these less obvious experiences can still have a severe impact on self-esteem.

Bad experiences may lead us to develop low self-esteem if we see them as signs of personal inadequacy, rather than as unfortunate events that could in theory happen to anyone. It is very important to bear in mind that our perceptions and beliefs can be inaccurate, as explained below.

Beliefs are not facts

Although our opinions of ourselves (i.e. **Bottom Line** beliefs) can be realistic, they can also be inaccurate, outdated, or completely false. This is not surprising when we remember that these beliefs start to form during early childhood, before we have much understanding of relationships and the world around us. For example, Tom had been a normal lively three year old, when his parents lost a baby and started to have major problems in their marriage. Consequently Tom's parents had less tolerance for his lively behaviour, and he was frequently shouted at and received little affection. Tom was not old enough to understand that his parents' excessive shouting and lack of affection was not his fault. He started to develop the **Bottom Line** belief that he was unacceptable.

Research has shown that young children commonly blame themselves for events that are clearly not their fault, such as their parents getting divorced, or childhood abuse. It is also possible for people to develop beliefs that make perfect sense of their childhood experiences, but then become unrealistic or outdated during adulthood. For example, a neglected child may understandably develop the belief "I'm not worth caring about". However, this belief may persist during adulthood despite the person having contact with people who are caring and supportive. This is because it is normal for our beliefs to be resistant to change. This resistance to change plays a key role in keeping low self-esteem going, and is explained in the next section.

KEY POINTS

- Low self-esteem is an understandable reaction to past experiences.
- It often stems from childhood but it can also develop during adulthood.
- The beliefs we develop about ourselves are opinions rather than facts, and can be inaccurate, outdated, or completely false.

2. What keeps the problem going?

This section explains how negative biases, unhelpful **Rules for Living** and self-defeating behaviours can keep low self-esteem going.

Negative biases

Psychologists have discovered that our beliefs tend to influence how we view, make sense of, and remember our daily experiences. In particular, we tend to view new events in ways that match our existing beliefs. This normal, automatic process may help us simplify the complex world around us, so that we can react quickly to new events and information. However, this process also makes our beliefs resistant to change, and problems may arise if the beliefs we develop are unrealistic.

Low self-esteem (i.e. overly negative **Bottom Line** beliefs) may lead people to ignore, discount, or forget positive information about themselves, such as strengths, achievements and compliments. It may also lead people to focus on negative things, such as weaknesses, mistakes and criticism. Ignoring the positives and focussing on the negatives strengthens overly negative **Bottom Line** beliefs, and stops people from developing more realistic beliefs.

Pam illustrates this process. Pam's childhood experiences have led her to develop the **Bottom Line** belief, "I'm unlovable". If anybody criticises her, or does not show her clear signs of friendliness, she automatically sees this as evidence that she is unlovable. On the other hand, when people are friendly and pay her compliments, she either does not notice, or she assumes that people are just being kind. It is easy to see how this process keeps Pam believing that she is unlovable.

Rules for Living

As with the **Bottom Line** beliefs, our **Rules for Living** are likely to be a reaction to our past experiences. We may develop certain rules to help us deal with and compensate for our **Bottom Line** beliefs. We may not be aware of these rules, and may not have put them into words before. However, we can usually work out what they are from observing our behaviour patterns. Some examples of **Rules for Living** are shown below.

	Bottom Line belief	**Rules for Living**
Rachel	I'm not good enough	If I work extremely hard at work and do everything perfectly then I can't be a complete failure
Tom	I'm unacceptable I'm not worth caring about	If I don't let anyone get to know what I'm really like then people might think I'm OK
Pam	I'm unlovable	If I please other people all the time then I might not be rejected
Adam	I'm stupid	If I don't try then I can't fail

Although these **Rules for Living** may have some pay-offs, such as making us feel better in the short-term, they can have disadvantages in the long-term (as illustrated in the examples on the next page). These rules can play a role in keeping low self-esteem going if they are unrealistic or too rigid. An example of an unrealistic and rigid rule is "I must always please other people no matter what". A more realistic and helpful alternative might be "I would like to be considerate to others most of the time".

Examples of short-term payoffs and long-term disadvantages

Rachel's rule leads her to put all her energy into her work. She feels great when she does well at work, but more often she feels stressed and exhausted. She neglects other areas of her life, and sees herself as a failure when she does not meet her unrealistic standards at work.

Tom's rule leads him to have little contact with other people, hide his feelings from others, and to avoid being himself. In the short-term this may reduce his anxiety about being rejected by other people. However, in the long-term it prevents him from discovering that people accept the "real Tom", and he remains anxious about letting his guard down.

Pam's rule means that she feels good when people praise her for her help and kindness. However, putting other people first all the time causes Pam to feel resentful at times and this makes her feel bad about herself. Her rule also stops her from realising that her true friends would still like her if she were more assertive and fairer to herself.

Adam's rule leads him to avoid challenges and opportunities to learn new skills. It helps him to deal with his fear of failure in the short-term. In the long run this rule stops him finding out what he can achieve, and therefore stops him building self-confidence.

Patterns that maintain low self-esteem

The patterns that are believed to keep self-esteem going are illustrated in the diagram on page 8. The diagrams on pages 9 and 10 show the patterns that maintain low self-esteem for Tom and Pam.

The top of the diagram suggests that past experiences lead to the development of **Bottom Line** beliefs. These beliefs may influence how we view, make sense of, and remember daily events, as well as our **Rules for Living**.

If the **Bottom Line** beliefs are overly negative then they may lead to negative biases in how we view, make sense of and remember events. These biases may cause us to ignore positive information about ourselves (strengths, achievements and compliments) and to focus on negative things (weaknesses, mistakes and criticism).

It is suggested that negative biases and unhelpful **Rules for Living** can lead to negative thoughts and self-defeating behaviours.

The bottom half of the diagram shows that negative thoughts can affect how we feel. Negative predictions (as shown above the dotted line) may lead to anxiety and self-defeating behaviours, such as avoiding things or taking unnecessary precautions. Such behaviours can stop us discovering the truth about our predictions. For example, when Tom is invited to a social event he predicts, “no one will want to talk to me”, and he feels anxious. This leads him to either avoid going to the social event, or to put on a façade and not let people see the “real Tom”. These behaviours are self-defeating because they stop Tom discovering that some people do want to talk to him, and that they like him when he is being himself.

Self-critical thoughts (as shown below the dotted line) may lead to depression, which in turn can lead to self-defeating behaviours, such as self-neglect, social withdrawal and inactivity. For example, Tom has self-critical thoughts such as “no one wants to know me” and this makes him feel depressed. Depression causes him to become more withdrawn, and his isolation makes him more convinced that no one wants to know him.

Self-defeating behaviours are likely to create more negative thoughts and stop us building more realistic **Bottom Line** beliefs.

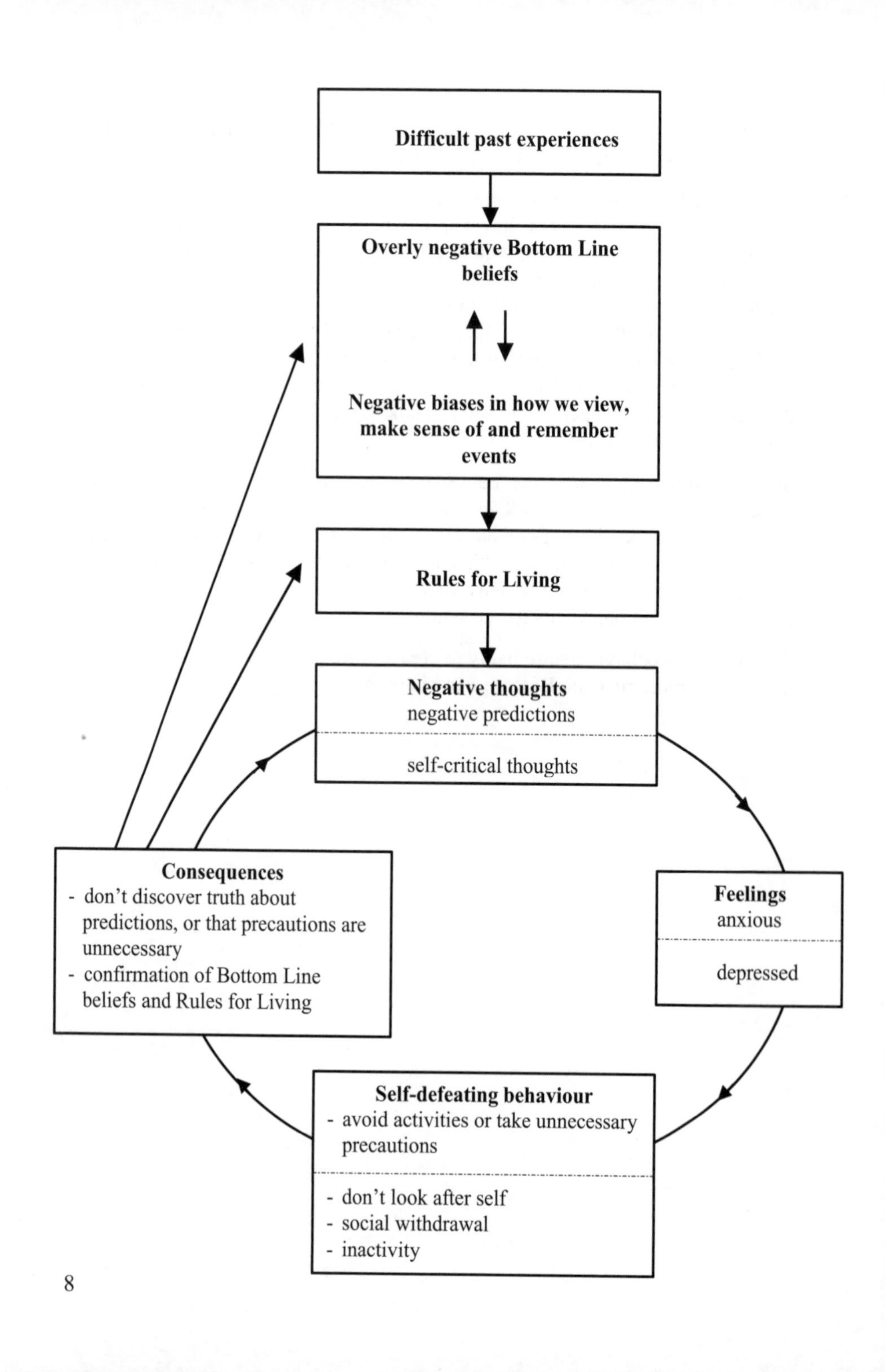
Difficult past experiences
Overly negative Bottom Line beliefs
Negative biases in how we view, make sense of and remember events
Rules for Living
Negative thoughts
negative predictions
self-critical thoughts
Feelings
anxious
depressed
Self-defeating behaviour
- avoid activities or take unnecessary precautions
- don't look after self
- social withdrawal
- inactivity
Consequences
- don't discover truth about predictions, or that precautions are unnecessary
- confirmation of Bottom Line beliefs and Rules for Living

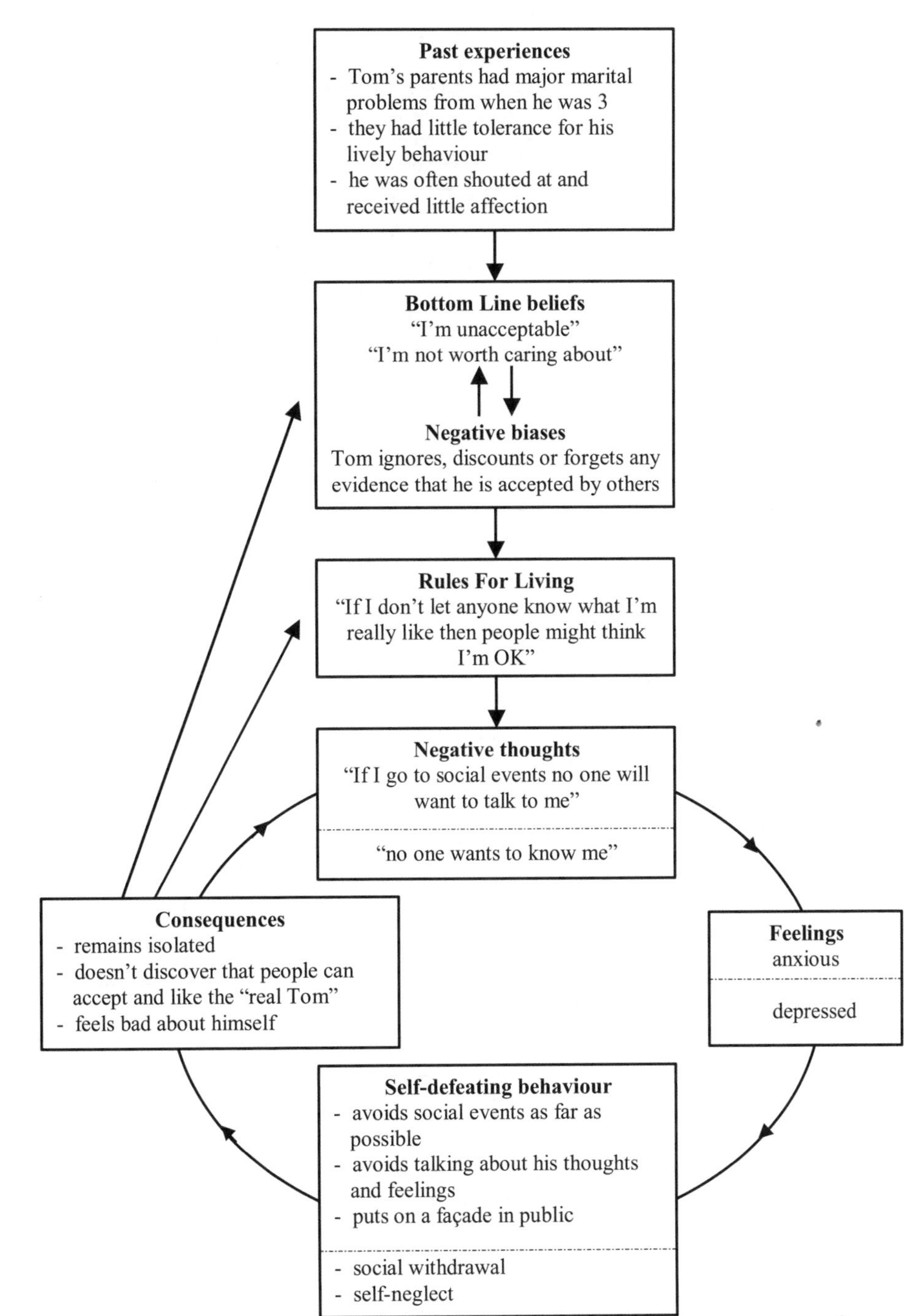
Past experiences
- Tom's parents had major marital problems from when he was 3
- they had little tolerance for his lively behaviour
- he was often shouted at and received little affection
Bottom Line beliefs
"I'm unacceptable"
"I'm not worth caring about"
Negative biases
Tom ignores, discounts or forgets any evidence that he is accepted by others
Rules For Living
"If I don't let anyone know what I'm really like then people might think I'm OK"
Negative thoughts
"If I go to social events no one will want to talk to me"
"no one wants to know me"
Feelings
anxious
depressed
Self-defeating behaviour
- avoids social events as far as possible
- avoids talking about his thoughts and feelings
- puts on a façade in public
- social withdrawal
- self-neglect
Consequences
- remains isolated
- doesn't discover that people can accept and like the "real Tom"
- feels bad about himself

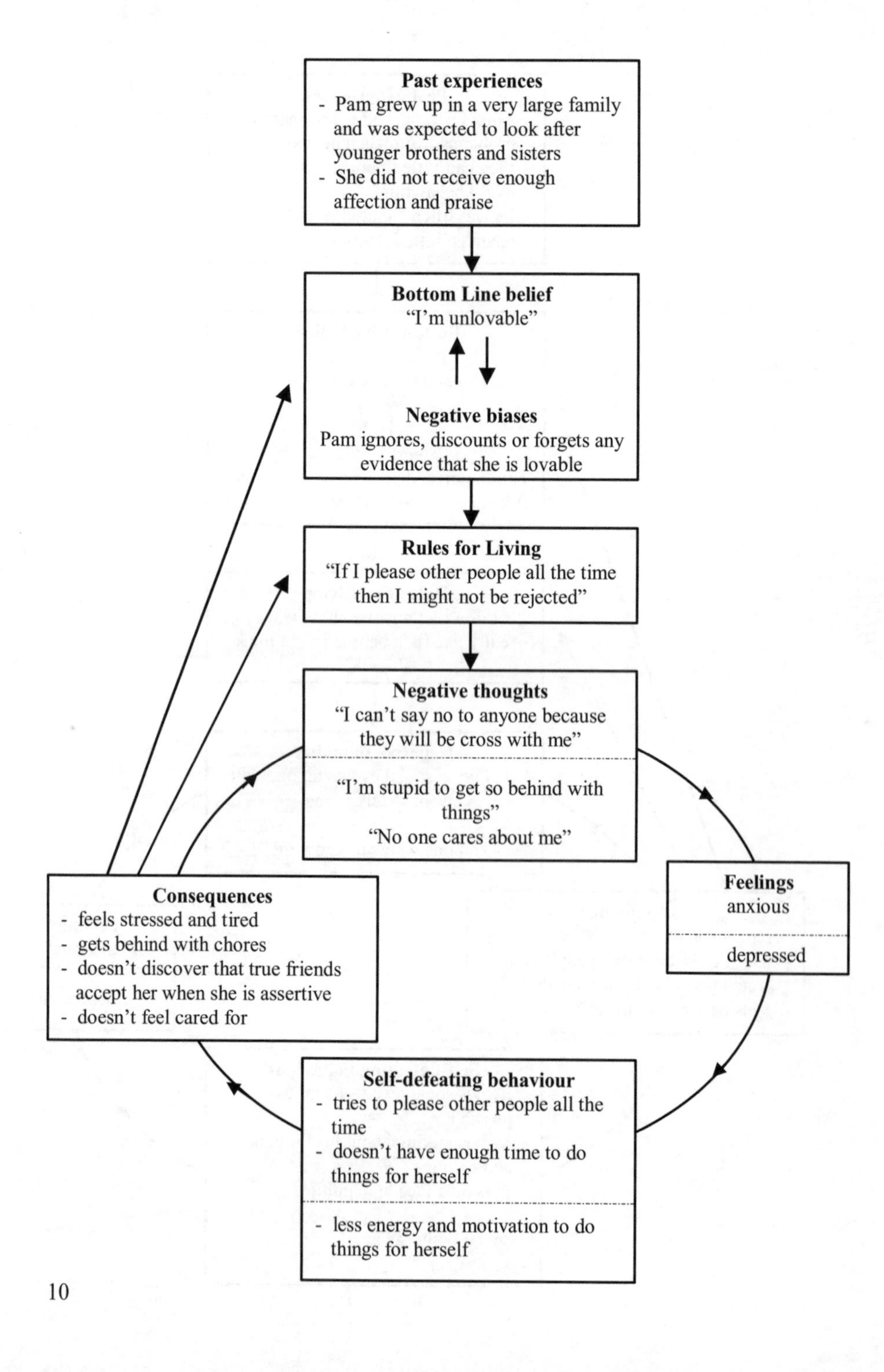
Past experiences
- Pam grew up in a very large family and was expected to look after younger brothers and sisters
- She did not receive enough affection and praise
Bottom Line belief
"I'm unlovable"
Negative biases
Pam ignores, discounts or forgets any evidence that she is lovable
Rules for Living
"If I please other people all the time then I might not be rejected"
Negative thoughts
"I can't say no to anyone because they will be cross with me"
"I'm stupid to get so behind with things"
"No one cares about me"
Feelings
anxious
depressed
Self-defeating behaviour
- tries to please other people all the time
- doesn't have enough time to do things for herself
- less energy and motivation to do things for herself
Consequences
- feels stressed and tired
- gets behind with chores
- doesn't discover that true friends accept her when she is assertive
- doesn't feel cared for

KEY POINTS

- Low self-esteem (i.e. overly negative **Bottom Line** beliefs) can cause people to ignore, discount, and forget positive information about themselves, and to focus on negative things.
- Low self-esteem can also lead people to develop unhelpful **Rules for Living** and self-defeating behaviours.
- These negative biases, unhelpful rules, and self-defeating behaviours can keep low self-esteem going.

3. Building self-esteem using CBT

The main aims of the CBT approach are to identify and break the unhelpful patterns that keep low self-esteem going, and to build more balanced and realistic beliefs. This involves recognising and overcoming the negative biases, unhelpful rules, and self-defeating behaviours. Methods for building self-esteem, and the reasons why they help, are outlined in the table below.

Method	**Rationale**
Activity diary	To help you improve your mood and self-esteem through planning more satisfying activities, looking after yourself better, and recognising your achievements on a daily basis.
Positives notebook	To help you notice and remember your positive qualities. This can help compensate for the tendency to ignore, discount and forget positive information about yourself, so that you can start to gain a more balanced view of yourself.
Thought record	To help you to become aware of and deal with biases in your thinking. This can improve how you feel, and help you build a more realistic view of yourself.
Behavioural experiments	Testing out negative thoughts in practice can be a powerful way of putting biased thinking in perspective. Experimenting with doing things differently can also help with overcoming unhelpful rules and self-defeating behaviours.

These CBT methods are described in detail below so that you can try them out for yourself. It is probably best to learn how to use one method at a time, and to use each method for a few weeks before deciding whether it seems to be helping you or not. Once you feel comfortable with one method you may then wish to introduce another one and so on. These CBT methods are most likely to be helpful if you can incorporate them into your life for **at least** a few months, rather than for just a few weeks. They may also be needed again in the future to help you deal with knocks to your confidence and setbacks.

Activity diary

The activity diary is an important part of CBT treatment for depression, and may be particularly valuable for people who experience depression as well as having low self-esteem. The purpose of this method is to help you to look after yourself better, to make your life more satisfying, and to give yourself credit for your daily achievements.

There are a number of different ways in which people with low self-esteem may neglect themselves. For example, Pam spends all her time helping other people; Rachel works so hard that she has virtually no time for relaxation and fun; and Tom neglects his health and appearance because he feels that he is not worth caring about. Not looking after yourself may reinforce low self-esteem, and make you more vulnerable to stress and depression.

Step 1: Keeping an activity diary

The first step is to look at how you spend your time, and to consider how satisfying you find your daily activities and routine. It can be helpful to do this in a systematic way using a diary sheet. An example of a completed activity diary is shown on page 13. You can draw up your own diary like the form on pages 16 and 17, and try filling it in for a week or so. It is best to fill it in as soon as you can after each activity. If you leave it more than a few hours it may be difficult to remember how you felt, and negative thinking may cloud how you remember the activity.

Time	Monday		
7-8 am	got children ready for school **P2 A6**	3-4 pm	collected children from school, looked after 2 other children **P2 A7** ↓
8-9 am	took children to school **P4 A2**	4-5 pm	
9-10 am	breakfast listening to radio **P7 A1,** tidied up **P1 A7**	5-6 pm	
10-11 am	at work, helped boss with ordering stock **P2 A5** ↓	6-7 pm	cooked dinner for everyone **P2 A5**, ate dinner **P6 A2**
11-12 pm		7-8 pm	got children ready for bed **P5 A5**
12-1 pm	listened to Sue's problems at lunchtime **P1 A7**	8-9 pm	tidied up **P0 A9**
1-2 pm	at work, served customers **P4 A6** ↓	9-10 pm	helped Mike with application form **P1 A8**
2-3 pm		10-11 pm	tried to read a book but fell asleep **P7 A1**

The idea is to record daily activities hour by hour, along with ratings of how satisfying you find each activity. Activities may be satisfying because they are pleasurable or because they give you a sense of achievement. The letter P and a number from 0 to 10 are used to indicate how pleasurable an activity was, with P0 indicating that an activity was not at all pleasurable, and P10 indicating that the activity was extremely pleasurable. Similarly the letter A and a number from 0 to 10 are used to indicate how much of an achievement an activity was.

With the achievement ratings it is important to take into account how you were feeling at the time, so that you give yourself credit for how much effort you put into the activity. For example, it may be easy to get out of bed when feeling well and looking forward to the day ahead, but this may be a struggle when feeling unwell on a difficult day, and would deserve a higher achievement rating. An example of what can go wrong is shown below.

Tom had been putting off going to the bank for months. He felt ashamed of his financial difficulties, and believed that the staff at the bank would be critical and disapproving. However, he gave himself an achievement rating of only 3 when he finally forced himself to go to the bank. His reasoning was "this should be easy - most people go to the bank without giving it a second thought". His achievement rating failed to take account of his personal circumstances, and the mental effort required to face something he feared. Not giving ourselves credit for the effort we put into things can reduce motivation, and keep depression and low self-esteem going.

Step 2: What would you like to change?

Once you have kept the diary for a week or so, it is time to reflect on how you spend your time and to consider what you would like to change. The following questions may help you with this.

- What was satisfying and what wasn't? What changes would you like to make in order to make your daily activities and routine more satisfying?
- Are you looking after yourself, and treating yourself as if you are a worthwhile person? If you were helping someone you cared about and wanted to treat well, what changes would you make?
- Are you striking a balance between enjoyable activities, relaxation, and things for yourself on the one hand, and work, duties, things for other people on the other? If not, what could you do to create a better balance?
- Are you able to acknowledge your daily achievements in the way someone else might? Low self-esteem and depression commonly lead people to discount their achievements. If this is a problem for you then further

practice in acknowledging achievements may be helpful. Remember to take into account how you felt at the time and how much effort was required for the activity.

- Was inactivity a problem for you? Depression and anxiety often lead people to become inactive and to avoid activities. This means that they are starved of enjoyment and a sense of achievement. Planning a gradual increase in your daily activities is one of the most powerful ways of improving energy levels and mood.
- Did negative thoughts get in the way of you doing things? If they did, write them down and try questioning them as described on page 21.

Time	Monday	Tuesday	Wednesday
7-8			
8-9			
9-10			
10-11			
11-12			
12-1			
1-2			
2-3			
3-4			
4-5			
5-6			
6-7			
7-8			
8-9			
9-10			
10-11			
11-12			

Thursday	Friday	Saturday	Sunday

Step 3: Making changes and planning activity

Once you have ideas about the kind of changes that you would like to make, the next stage involves trying this out in practice. This can be done by looking at the week ahead, scheduling achievable activities for each day, and planning a more satisfying routine for yourself. Plan half a day at a time, or even a whole day if you can. Aim for a pattern that will work for you. If that seems too much, however, then start with something more manageable. Even one small change a day will make a difference, and you can use it as a basis for gradually increasing enjoyment and achievement. Once you have tried making changes, you can review the impact of these changes. If the changes lead to an increase in your levels of enjoyment and achievement, then you can build on the changes you have made. If the changes turn out to be unhelpful, you can work out what went wrong, and take this information into account when you plan further changes.

Positives notebook

The negative biases that play a role in maintaining low self-esteem were described on page 4. You may remember how Pam takes to heart any negative comments she receives, and ignores or discounts the times when people are friendly towards her or pay her compliments. The positives notebook is a way of compensating for these biases, so that you can develop a more accepting and balanced opinion of yourself.

Step 1: Identifying positive qualities

People with low self-esteem are generally out of the habit of spotting their own positive qualities and strengths, and therefore you are likely to find this difficult initially. The following questions may help you to become more aware of your positive qualities. When going through these questions look out for any negative thoughts that lead you to discount your positive qualities, such as "that's nothing special" or "I could have done it better". These are examples of your negative biases at work. Try not to let them stop you writing down your positive qualities.

- Is there anything that you like about yourself, however insignificant it seems?
- What are the positive achievements of your life so far, however modest? Have you maintained any friendships, held down a job, been a parent or a carer, or developed any skills related to your job, domestic life, leisure activities and interests? For example, do you know how to cook, drive, ride

a bicycle, swim, sew, use a computer, and do housework, gardening or DIY? Do you have any academic, artistic, sporting or people skills?

- What obstacles have you tried to overcome? Give yourself credit for the efforts you have made to overcome problems and anxieties, as this often requires courage and determination.
- What would someone who cares about you, and is on your side, say your qualities and strengths are? You could try asking someone for help with this, but be careful not to ask someone who may have contributed to your low self-esteem (for example, a critical parent or partner).
- What qualities and strengths do you appreciate in other people? Do you have any of these qualities and strengths yourself to any degree?
- What negative qualities do you NOT have? If you can name some negative qualities you do not have (for example being cruel or abusive) then this suggests that you must have positive qualities (for example, being caring or respectful).

An example of Tom's list of qualities, strengths and achievements is as follows:

- I did not have an easy time as a child because my parents didn't get on, and I didn't get much support or encouragement from them. My unhappiness as a child made it difficult for me to settle in at school. I felt like giving up at school, but I tried hard during my last year and managed to pass a few exams, and I did better than people predicted. <u>I have determination.</u>
- I have done OK at work and have been promoted. My colleagues sometimes ask for my advice, and I received a good reference from my old job. <u>I am competent and knowledgeable at work.</u>
- I have a few friends, a couple of whom I have known for many years. Also a teacher and a neighbour seemed to like me when I was a child. <u>I am likeable.</u>
- I have learnt how to use a computer, cook, drive, swim, and play squash. <u>I have skills.</u>
- <u>I am usually punctual and reliable.</u>
- I take good care of my dog. <u>I am caring.</u>

Write down your positive qualities in a notebook, leaving room so that you can add to the list as new things occur to you. In order to bring this alive, look at the list and remember as vividly as you can, the times when you have shown these qualities in the past, and note down these examples. After a few days when you think that you have got as far as you can with the list, the next step is to look for evidence of these qualities on a daily basis. You may have been ignoring and discounting your positive qualities for a very long time. Daily practice at spotting your positive qualities will help this become more automatic.

Step 2: Daily recording of positive qualities

Write down any evidence of your positive qualities and strengths on a daily basis. Try to write down at least three each day. If three is too many, then start out with two or one. Even this may be difficult initially, but it should become easier with practice. (If you are keeping an activity diary this may help you identify your daily achievements.) The idea is to keep this going until you get into the habit of identifying your positive qualities, and can spot several each day without too much difficulty. It may take a few months until this becomes more automatic, or longer if the problem of low self-esteem is particularly severe and longstanding. An example of a page from a positives notebook is shown below.

Date	**Evidence of positive quality**	**Positive quality**
9.10.03	Let another driver into queue of traffic	Considerate
	Colleagues asked me to join them for lunch	likeable
	Dealt with angry customer without losing my cool	competent
10.10.03	Sorted out computer problem for colleague	helpful, skilled
	Colleagues asked me to join them for lunch again	likeable
	Took dog for a walk despite feeling tired	caring
	Nervous about not knowing anyone at evening class but went anyway	courageous

Notice that the record does not just list the quality (for example, "was considerate"), but gives a little bit of detail. If you do this, you will be able to look back over your positives notebook and remember what is described in it. This will counter your tendency to forget good things about yourself, and give you a store of good memories to call on when you are feeling low or discouraged. It is important to note that none of the examples is earth shattering and that small things count. Beware of ignoring or discounting things because you think they are "trivial" or "nothing special"; or because you have written down something similar already.

Thought record

Low self-esteem can lead people to make anxious predictions and to be overly self-critical. The thought record can help you become more aware of anxious predictions and self-criticism. You can then question and test out these negative thoughts, rather than assuming that they are 100 percent true. This can help break the unhelpful patterns in thinking and behaviour that keep low self-esteem going.

Again this method will take some time to get used to. An example of a thought record is shown on page 23, and there is a step-by-step guide to using this method below.

Step 1: Recording negative thoughts and feelings

- You can draw up a record form like the one on page 23, leaving plenty of room to write in the columns. It helps to write down your thoughts and feelings as soon as you can, so you will need to carry a record form or notebook with you. Make sure your record is easy to carry.
- The idea is to look out for times when you feel particularly distressed. It may not be practical or helpful to write down every distressing event. You may want to focus on the worst few times, or a few typical examples, so that you are not writing down more than three examples each day.
- In the "situation" column write down what you were doing when you began to feel upset.
- In the "emotion" column try to write down the main emotions you felt. (Emotions are usually single words such as anxious, sad, depressed, angry, embarrassed, ashamed, or frustrated.) It can sometimes be difficult to put emotions into words. Have a go at doing this as far as you can, then move on to the column for "negative thoughts".
- Try to catch what was going through your mind when you became distressed and write this down in the "negative thoughts" column. What was it about the situation that distressed you? Did it trigger any self-critical or anxious thoughts, or any distressing images or memories? Try to put

these thoughts, images and memories into words and write them down as shown on the next page.

- Once you have got into the habit of catching negative thoughts and feelings, perhaps after a week of practice, the next step is to question these thoughts and to look for a balanced and realistic perspective, as described below.

Step 2: Questioning negative thoughts

The following questions may help you with the process of questioning negative thoughts, and coming to a balanced perspective.

- What is the evidence supporting this thought? What is the evidence against it?
- What alternative perspectives are there? What would you say to a friend if they were in your shoes, and were having thoughts like these? What might a friend say to you if they knew you were thinking in this way? Is there any evidence for these alternative perspectives?
- Are you predicting the future? If so, what is the worst that could happen? What is the best that could happen? What is most likely to happen? If the worst happens what could be done about it?
- Are there any biases or errors in your thinking? Are you mind reading or jumping to conclusions? Are you thinking in all-or-nothing terms, or expecting perfection of yourself? Are you focussing on your weaknesses and forgetting your strengths?
- What are the pros and cons of thinking in this way?

Situation	Emotions	Negative thoughts	Balanced thoughts
Boss pointed out mistakes in my work	sad	I'm totally useless, I can't do my job	Everyone makes mistakes sometimes. Making a few mistakes doesn't necessarily mean I'm useless. If I were terrible at my job my boss would have told me or sacked me
Phil didn't invite me out	sad angry	Phil doesn't want to spend time with me	Phil may not have known I was free this weekend. Even if he did, he may have had other plans. This is not hard evidence that Phil doesn't like me
Told about new computer system at work	anxious	I won't be able to learn how to use the new computer system. I will have to resign	I haven't tried to use it yet, so I might be jumping to conclusions
Forgot a meeting with son's teacher	guilty anxious	I'm a bad mother. The teacher will think I'm a bad mother	This is the first time I've forgotten a meeting concerning my son. I try hard to do my best for my children. If the teacher thinks I'm a bad mother she is wrong

Behavioural experiments

Behavioural experiments take the thought record one important step further, by testing out negative thoughts in practice. It is a good idea to keep a record of behavioural experiments, as shown on page 25. There is a step-by-step guide to recording behavioural experiments below.

1. The first step is to write down your negative thoughts in the first column. These thoughts may come from your thought record.
2. The next step is to think about how you might test out your negative thoughts, and to write down this plan of action in the "Experiment" column.
3. Before carrying out your experiment, write down what you predict will happen in the "Prediction" column.
4. Once you have carried out the experiment, write down whether your prediction was correct and what actually happened.
5. Finally, compare your prediction with what actually happened, and write down what you have learnt in the "Conclusions" column.

Keeping a written record of behavioural experiments can help you find out whether your predictions tend to be realistic or whether they are being affected by negative biases. If your predictions tend to be overly negative then testing them out in practice can be a powerful way of putting them in perspective.

However, even if your predictions tend to be overly negative, it is still possible that they will be accurate at times. If you receive negative feedback following an experiment, try not to let it become distorted out of proportion. Completing a thought record may help you keep negative feedback in perspective.

Negative thoughts	Experiment	Prediction	What actually happened?	Conclusions
My boss pointed out mistakes therefore I'm not good enough at my job	Ask boss for feedback on my performance	She will tell me that I'm not good enough	She said that she is happy with my work in general	Perhaps I'm more competent than I give myself credit for
Phil doesn't like me because he didn't invite me out at the weekend	I could ask him if he would like to meet up one night this week	He will make some excuse	He suggested meeting up on Friday, and seemed friendly	Maybe Phil thinks I'm OK. I was jumping to conclusions
I will never be able to learn how to use the new computer system	I could ask Jane whether she would explain it to me	I won't be able to take in anything Jane tells me	I remembered most of what I was told. I still needed a bit of help the next time I used it, but I'm learning	It wasn't as hard to learn as I thought it would be. I tend to underestimate my abilities
My son's teacher will think that I'm a bad mother for forgetting our appointment	Contact teacher to apologise and explain	She will be cross with me and unfriendly	She just said "no problem" and didn't seem to have time to talk	She might be cross with me, or perhaps she was just in a hurry? At least I apologised

Behavioural experiments can also be used to tackle unhelpful **Rules for Living** and self-defeating behaviours. The table below shows some examples of unhelpful **Rules for Living** and self-defeating behaviours, along with ideas for tackling these using behavioural experiments.

Rules for Living	**Self-defeating behaviours**	**Ideas for experiments**
Rachel's rule: If I work extremely hard at work and do everything perfectly then I can't be a complete failure	Rachel puts all her energy into her work and neglects other areas of her life	Rachel could set limits on how much time she spends working, and ask for feedback on whether her work is still good enough
Tom's rule: If I don't let anyone get to know what I'm really like then people might think I'm OK	Tom has little contact with other people and avoids being himself	Tom could experiment with having more contact with people, and talking a little bit more about himself. He could observe whether people accept him
Pam's rule: If I please other people all the time then I might not be rejected	Pam puts other people first all the time and neglects her own needs	Pam could experiment with putting time aside for activities she wants to do. She could say no to some requests from others, and see how they react
Adam's rule: If I don't try then I can't fail	Adam avoids challenges and opportunities to learn new skills	Adam could try learning a new skill to see if he makes any progress

If you have become aware of any unhelpful rules or self-defeating behaviours, you may wish to experiment with doing things differently. This can be challenging and anxiety provoking, so it is probably best to start with something relatively small, and to make changes one step at a time. For example, Rachel might start with not taking work home with her at weekends, and planning to do rewarding leisure activities instead. She may be able to assess whether her work is still good enough by seeing whether she receives complaints, and by seeking feedback from a colleague. Her record of this experiment might look as follows.

Self-defeating behaviour	Experiment	Prediction	What actually happened?	Conclusions
Working too hard	Stop working at weekends for one month, plan enjoyable activities instead, ask my colleague (Sam) for feedback	My work won't be good enough, my colleagues will notice and complain	I received no complaints, Sam said he thought that my work had been fine, and I have felt more energetic	When I don't work at weekends, my work can still be good enough, and I feel more energetic

Once Rachel feels more comfortable with not working at weekends, she may then decide to experiment with not working so late in the evenings, and so on.

Maintaining improvement

The CBT self-help methods described in this booklet may help you overcome the negative biases, unhelpful rules and self-defeating behaviours that keep low self-esteem going. In view of the fact that low self-esteem can be a longstanding and resistant problem, it may be necessary to keep using these self-help methods over a period of several months. It is also important to be prepared to start using these methods again in the future, to help you deal with setbacks.

KEY POINTS

- The CBT methods for building self-esteem include the activity diary, the positives notebook, the thought record, and behavioural experiments.
- These methods involve planning more satisfying activities and looking after yourself; overcoming self-defeating behaviours; compensating for

negative biases, by learning to notice and record your positive qualities and achievements; and learning to question and test out negative thoughts.

- These methods are most likely to be helpful if you can incorporate them into your life for **at least** a few months, and if you are able to keep using them whenever you experience a setback.

---

4. Further reading

If you would like to read more about CBT self-help methods you may find the following books helpful.

- Overcoming low self-esteem, by Melanie Fennell (1999). Robinson Publishing Ltd: London. (A detailed and comprehensive account of CBT for low self-esteem.)
- Overcoming low self-esteem self-help course (3 parts), Melanie Fennell (2006). Robinson Publishing Ltd: London. (Similar to the above, but in an easy to use workbook style)
- Self-esteem, by Matthew McKay & Patrick Fanning (1992). New Harbinger Publications: California.
- 10 days to great self-esteem, by David Burns (2000). Published by Vermilion.
- Overcoming childhood trauma, by Helen Kennerley (2000). Robinson Publishing Ltd: London.
- Overcoming shyness and social anxiety, by Gillian Butler (1999). Robinson Publishing Ltd: London.
- Overcoming depression, by Paul Gilbert (1997). Robinson Publishing Ltd: London.
- Manage Your Mind, by Gillian Butler & Tony Hope (1995). Oxford University Press: Oxford (2nd edition forthcoming soon, 2006).
- The Feeling Good Handbook (revised edition), by David Burns (1999). Published by Penguin.
- Mind Over Mood, by Dennis Greenberger & Christine Padesky (1995). Guilford Press: New York.

5. Getting professional help

If you want to get further help with your depression, and you are not already seeing a mental health professional, you need to talk to your GP to discuss what kind of referral might be possible and appropriate. For further advice on medication, you will need to see a psychiatrist. Psychological treatments, like CBT or IPT, may be offered by a number of different members of the mental health team. Unfortunately a lack of NHS resources means that there are often very long waiting lists for psychological treatments. Your GP will be able to advise you on what treatments are available in your area and what the waiting time is likely to be.

If you are considering getting therapy independently, the British Association for Behavioural and Cognitive Psychotherapies (BABCP) has a directory of accredited CBT therapists. These are people who have had approved training and supervision in CBT You can find out about accredited therapists by visiting the BABCP website at www.babcp.com and clicking on 'Find a therapist'.

6. OCTC

For a full list of other Oxford Cognitive Therapy Centre booklets about a variety of problems, visit our website at www.octc.co.uk or contact us at:

OCTC
Warneford Hospital
Oxford
OX3 7JX

Tel: 01865 738 816
Fax: 01865 738 817
Email: octc@oxfordhealth.nhs.uk

Booklets from OCTC that you may find helpful include:

- Managing depression, by David Westbrook
- Overcoming social anxiety, by Gillian Butler

7. Acknowledgements

Many people have helped with the writing of this booklet. We would particularly like to thank the patients who kindly provided very important feedback; and our colleagues, Helen Kennerley and Gillian Butler, for making very helpful comments on an earlier draft. The CBT methods described in this booklet have been strongly influenced by the pioneering work of other therapists, including Professor Tim Beck, Dr Christine Padesky, and Professor Paul Gilbert.